ENERGY STAR

Change the World,
Start with ENERGY STAR®

The average household spends more than $2,200 a year on energy bills, with nearly half of this going to heating and cooling costs. The U.S. Environmental Protection Agency (EPA) can help you make smart decisions about your home's heating, ventilating, and air conditioning (HVAC) system that can help save on energy costs, improve your overall comfort at home, and help fight global warming.

Did you know the energy used in the average house is responsible for twice as many greenhouse gas emissions as the average car?

When power plants burn fossil fuels to make electricity, they release greenhouse gases. By using less energy at home, you help reduce the emissions that contribute to global warming.

ENERGY STAR is the government-backed program that helps us all save money and protect our environment with energy-efficient products and practices. Whether you are looking for recommendations about energy-efficient equipment, getting a quality installation, HVAC maintenance, or ways to make your heating and cooling system operate more efficiently, EPA's ENERGY STAR program can help.

Contents

....

Why Read this Guide?

Use this guide to help you:

☐ Learn how best to maintain your heating and cooling equipment.

☐ Take steps around your home to improve the efficiency of your HVAC system.

☐ Decide when it's time to replace your old heating and cooling equipment with more energy-efficient equipment that has earned EPA's ENERGY STAR.

Consider Making a Change if Any of the Following Statements Apply

☐ **Some of your rooms are too hot or cold.** Inadequate air sealing or insufficient insulation could be the cause. No matter how efficient your heating and cooling system is, if your home is not properly sealed and insulated, you will not be as comfortable and your system will have to work harder. Learn more about how to "Seal and Insulate with ENERGY STAR" on page 12.

☐ **Your home has humidity problems, excessive dust, or rooms that never seem to get comfortable.** Leaky or poorly insulated ductwork might be the cause. See "Seal Your Heating and Cooling Ducts" on page 10.

☐ **Your equipment needs frequent repairs and your energy bills are going up.** In addition to the rise in energy costs, the age and condition of your heating and cooling equipment may have caused it to become less efficient. See "Maintain Your Equipment" on page 6 or "Making a Change? Choose the Right Equipment" on page 16.

☐ **Your heating and cooling equipment is more than 10 years old.** Consider replacing it with newer, more efficient equipment. And remember, high efficiency levels begin with ENERGY STAR. See "Making a Change? Choose the Right Equipment" on page 16.

☐ **You leave your thermostat set at one constant temperature.** You could be missing a great energy-saving opportunity. You can set a programmable thermostat to adjust your home's temperature at times when you're regularly away or sleeping. See "Use a Programmable Thermostat Properly" on page 8.

☐ **You used EPA's ENERGY STAR Home Energy Yardstick (www.energystar. gov/yardstick) to compare your household's energy use to others across the country and your score is below five.** That means you're using and paying for more energy at home than most Americans. Visit the ENERGY STAR Home Advisor (www.energystar.gov/homeadvisor) to get recommendations for home improvement projects that will increase your score by improving your home's energy efficiency and comfort.

ENERGY STAR

Maintain Your Equipment

Dirt and neglect are the top causes of heating and cooling system inefficiency and failure. To ensure efficient system operation, it's important to perform routine maintenance.

Change your air filter regularly. A clean filter will prevent dust and dirt from building up in the system, which can lead to expensive maintenance and/or early system failure. Check your filter every month, especially during winter and summer months, when use tends to be heavier. Change your filter if it's dirty— or at least every three months.

Tune up your HVAC equipment. Proper maintenance by a qualified technician is one of the most important steps you can take to prevent future problems. Contractors get busy during summer and winter months, so it is best to check the cooling system in spring and the heating system in the fall. Plan the check-ups around the beginning and end of daylight-saving time each spring and fall. For tips on hiring the right contractor, see page 18, "Work with a Heating and Cooling Contractor."

Overall System Maintenance Checklist
Your contractor should complete the following each spring and fall:

- [ ] **Check thermostat settings** to ensure the heating and cooling system turns on and off at the programmed temperatures.

- [ ] **Tighten all electrical connections and measure voltage and current on motors.** Faulty electrical connections can cause your system to operate unsafely and reduce the life of major components.

- [ ] **Lubricate moving parts.** Parts that lack lubrication cause friction in motors and increase the amount of electricity you use. Lack of lubrication can also cause equipment to wear out more quickly, requiring more frequent repairs or replacements.

- [ ] **Check and inspect the condensate drain in your central air conditioner, furnace, and/or heat pump (when in cooling mode).** If plugged, the drain can cause water damage in the house, affect indoor humidity levels, and breed bacteria and mold.

☐ Check system controls to ensure proper and safe operation. Check the starting cycle of the equipment to assure the system starts, operates, and shuts off properly.

☐ Inspect, clean, or change the air filter in your central air conditioner, furnace, and/or heat pump. Your contractor can show you how to do this yourself. Depending on your system, your filter may be located in the duct system versus the heating and cooling equipment itself.

Additional System-Specific Maintenance Activities

For Heating Systems:

☐ Inspect the flue piping for rusting and any disconnections or evidence of back drafting.

☐ Check all gas (or oil) connections, gas pressure, burner combustion, and heat exchanger. Improper burner operation can be caused by a dirty burner or a cracked heat exchanger—either can cause the equipment to operate less safely and efficiently. Leaking gas (or oil) connections are also a fire hazard and can contribute to health problems.

For Cooling Systems:

☐ Clean indoor and outdoor coils before warm weather starts. A dirty coil reduces the system's ability to cool your home and causes the system to run longer, increasing your energy costs and shortening the life of your equipment.

☐ Check your central air conditioner's refrigerant charge and adjust it if necessary to make sure it meets manufacturer specifications. Too much or too little refrigerant charge can damage the compressor, reducing the life of your equipment and increasing costs.

☐ Clean and adjust blower components to provide proper system airflow. Proper airflow over the indoor coil is necessary for efficient equipment operation and reliability.

Use a Programmable Thermostat Properly

A programmable thermostat is ideal for people who are away from home during set periods of time throughout the week. Through proper use of pre-programmed settings, a programmable thermostat can save you about $180 every year in energy costs.

How Do You Choose the Right One for You?

To decide which model is best for you, think about your schedule and how often you are away from home for regular periods of time—work, school, other activities—and then decide which of the three different models best fits your schedule:

7-day models are best if your daily schedule tends to change; for example, if children are at home earlier on some days. These models give you the most flexibility and let you set different programs for different days—usually with four possible temperature periods per day.

5+2-day models use the same schedule every weekday, and another for weekends.

5-1-1 models are best if you tend to keep one schedule Monday through Friday and another schedule on Saturdays and Sundays.

Programmable Thermostat Settings

You can use the table below as a starting point for setting energy-saving temperatures, and then adjust the settings to fit your family's schedule and stay comfortable.

Setting	Time	Setpoint Temperature (Heat)	Setpoint Temperature (Cool)
Wake	6:00 a.m.	< 70° F	> 78° F
Day	8:00 a.m.	Setback at least 8° F	Setup at least 7° F
Evening	6:00 p.m.	< 70° F	> 78° F
Sleep	10:00 p.m.	Setback at least 8° F	Setup at least 4° F

Get the Greatest Benefit from Your Programmable Thermostat

☐ Install your thermostat away from heating or cooling registers, appliances, lighting, doorways, fireplaces, skylights and windows, and areas that receive direct sunlight or drafts. Interior walls are best.

☐ Keep the thermostat set at energy-saving temperatures for long periods of time, such as during the day when no one is home and at bedtime.

☐ Set the "hold" button at a constant energy-saving temperature when going away for the weekend or on vacation.

☐ Resist the urge to override the pre-programmed settings. Every time you do, you use more energy and may end up paying more on your energy bill.

☐ Use a programmable thermostat for each zone of your house if you have multiple heating and cooling zones. This will help you maximize comfort, convenience, and energy savings throughout the house.

☐ Change your batteries each year if your programmable thermostat runs on batteries. Some units will indicate when batteries must be changed.

If you have a heat pump, you may require a special programmable thermostat to maximize your energy savings year-round. Talk to your retailer or contractor for details before selecting your thermostat.

If you have a manual thermostat, you can adjust the temperatures daily before you leave the house and when you go to sleep at night. Typically, adjusting temperatures 5 – 8 degrees (down in winter, up in summer) can help save energy if you are going to be away from home for several hours.

Seal Your Heating and Cooling Ducts

Ducts are used to distribute conditioned air throughout houses with forced-air heating and cooling systems. In typical houses, about 20 percent of the air that moves through the duct system is lost due to leaks, holes, and poorly connected ducts. The result is an inefficient HVAC system, high utility bills, and difficulty keeping the house comfortable, no matter how the thermostat is set.

Simple Steps to Improving Duct Performance

Because ducts are often concealed in walls, ceilings, attics, and basements, repairing them can be difficult. But there are things that you can do to improve duct performance in your house.

Start by sealing leaks using mastic sealant or metal (foil) tape and insulating all the ducts that you can access such as those in the attic, crawlspace, basement, or garage. Never use 'duct tape,' as it is not long-lasting.

Also make sure that the connections at vents and registers are well-sealed where they meet the floors, walls, and ceiling. These are common locations to find leaks and disconnected ductwork.

Working with a Contractor

Many homeowners choose to hire a professional contractor for duct improvement projects. Most heating and cooling contractors also repair ductwork. Look for a contractor who will:

☐ Inspect the whole duct system, including the attic, basement, and crawlspace (if you have these).

☐ Evaluate the system's supply and return air balance. Many systems have air return ducts that are too small.

☐ Repair or replace damaged, disconnected, or undersized ducts and straighten out flexible ducts that are tangled or crushed.

☐ Seal leaks and connections with mastic, metal tape, or an aerosol-based sealant.

- [ ] Seal gaps behind registers and grills where the duct meets the floor, wall, or ceiling.

- [ ] Insulate ducts in unconditioned areas with insulation that carries an R-value of 6 or higher.

- [ ] Include a new filter as part of any duct system improvement.

- [ ] Use diagnostic tools to evaluate air flow after repairs are completed.

- [ ] Ensure there is no back drafting of gas or oil-burning appliances, and conduct a combustion safety test after ducts are sealed.

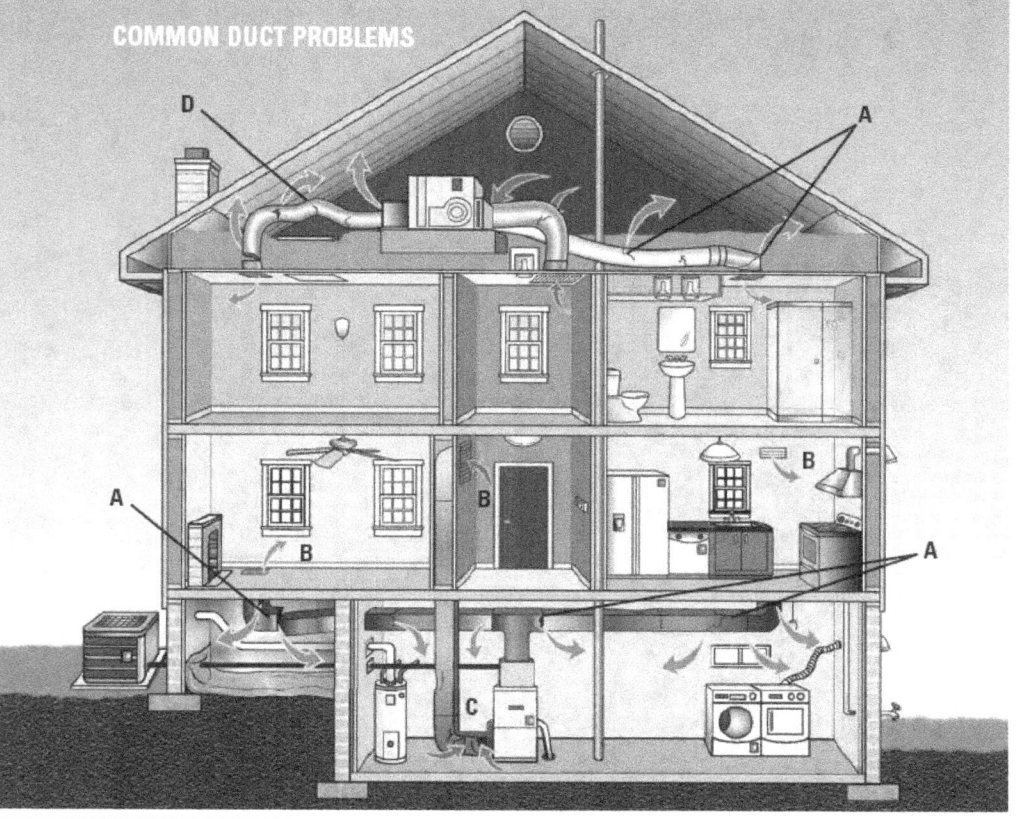

COMMON DUCT PROBLEMS

A Leaky, torn, and disconnected ducts

B Poorly sealed registers and grills

C Leaks at furnace and filter slot

D Kinks in flexible ductwork restricting airflow

Seal and Insulate with ENERGY STAR

The exterior of your home—the outer walls, ceiling, windows, and floor—is called the "envelope" or "shell." As a knowledgeable homeowner or with the help of a skilled contractor, you can save up to 20 percent on heating and cooling costs (or up to 10 percent on your total annual energy bill) by sealing and insulating your home envelope. It will also make your home more comfortable and help your heating and cooling system run more efficiently.

To improve your home's envelope, you can make these changes yourself:

If your attic is accessible and you like home improvement projects, you can Do-It-Yourself with help from EPA's DIY Guide to Sealing and Insulating with ENERGY STAR.

The Guide offers step-by-step instructions for sealing common air leaks and adding insulation to the attic to block heat loss in winter and heat gain in summer.

You can also hire a contractor who will use special diagnostic tools to pinpoint and seal the hidden air leaks in your home. A Home Energy Rater can help you find contractors that offer air sealing services in your area.

Hidden Air Leaks

Be sure to look for and seal air leaks before you install insulation because it performs best when air is not moving through or around it. Many air leaks and drafts are easy to find because they are easy to feel—like those around windows and doors. But holes hidden in attics, basements, and crawlspaces are usually bigger problems. Sealing these leaks with caulk, spray foam, or weather stripping will have a great impact on improving your comfort and reducing utility bills.

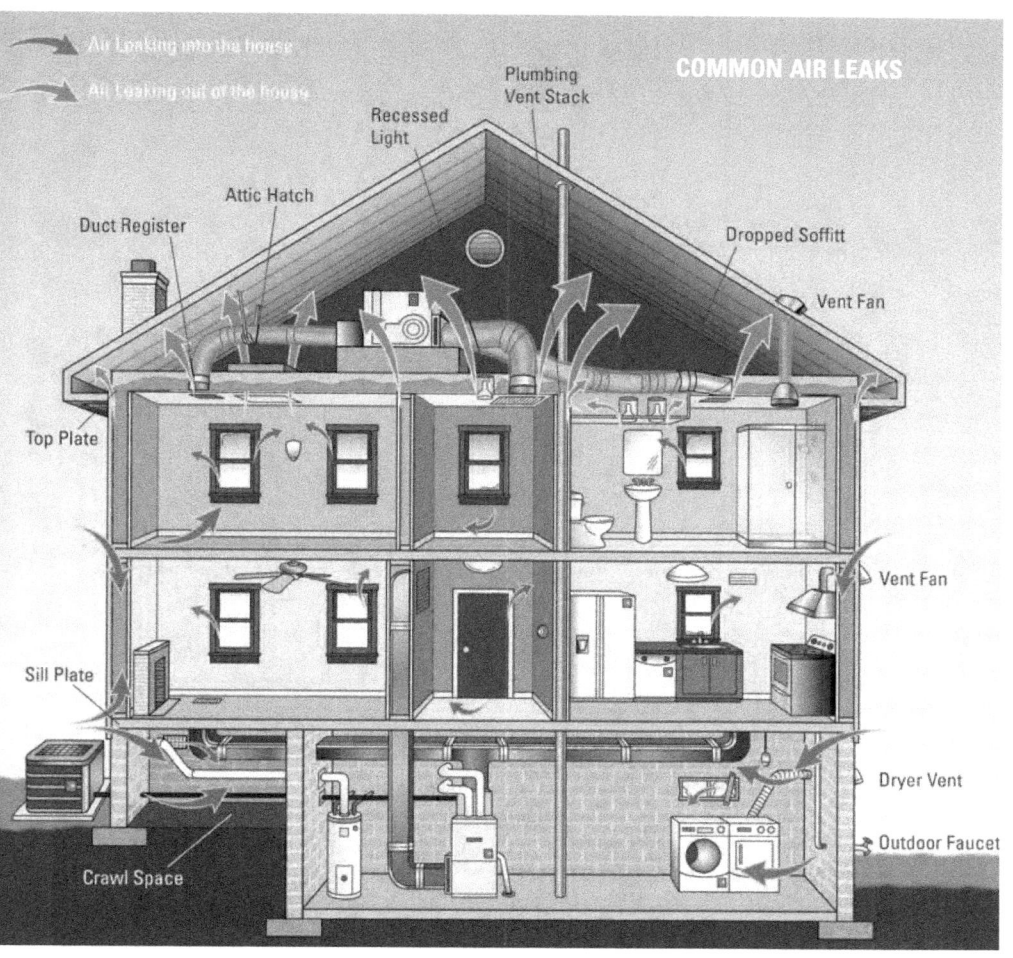

COMMON AIR LEAKS

Air Leaking into the house
Air Leaking out of the house

- Plumbing Vent Stack
- Recessed Light
- Attic Hatch
- Duct Register
- Dropped Soffitt
- Vent Fan
- Top Plate
- Vent Fan
- Sill Plate
- Dryer Vent
- Outdoor Faucet
- Crawl Space

Homeowners are often concerned about sealing their house too tightly; however, this is very unlikely in many older homes. A certain amount of fresh air is needed for good indoor air quality, and there are specifications that set the minimum amount of fresh air needed for a house. If you are concerned about how tight your home is, hire a contractor, such as a Home Energy Rater, who can use diagnostic tools to measure your home's actual air leakage. If your home is too tight, a fresh air ventilation system may be recommended.

After any project where you reduce air leakage, have a heating and cooling technician check to make sure that your combustion appliances (gas- or oil-fired furnace, water heater, and dryer) are venting properly. For additional information on Indoor Air Quality (IAQ) issues related to homes, such as combustion safety, visit EPA's Indoor Air Quality Web site at www.epa.gov/iaq.

Adding Insulation

Insulation keeps your home warm in the winter and cool in the summer. There are several common types of insulation—fiberglass (in both batt and blown forms), cellulose, rigid foam board, and spray foam. Reflective insulation (or radiant barrier) is another insulating product that can help save energy in hot, sunny climates. When correctly installed with air sealing, each type of insulation can deliver comfort and lower energy bills during the hottest and coldest times of the year.

Insulation performance is measured by R-value—its ability to resist heat flow. Higher R-values mean more insulating power. Different R-values are recommended for walls, attics, basements, and crawlspaces, depending on your area of the country. Insulation works best when air is not moving through or around it, making it very important to seal air leaks before installing insulation to ensure that you get the best performance from the insulation.

To get the biggest savings, the easiest place to add insulation is usually in the attic. A quick way to see if you need more insulation is to look across your uncovered attic floor. If your insulation is level with or below the attic floor joists, you probably need to add more. The recommended insulation level for most attics is R-38 (or about 12 – 15 inches, depending on the insulation type). In the coldest climates, insulating up to R-49 is recommended.

ENERGY STAR Qualified Windows

Windows are an important part of your home's envelope. ENERGY STAR qualified windows feature advanced technologies such as invisible glass coatings, vacuum-sealed spaces filled with inert gas between the panes, improved framing materials, better weather stripping, and warm edge spacers, all of which reduce undesirable heat gain and loss.

Increase savings. With more efficient windows, you can save money and use less energy. Installing ENERGY STAR qualified windows can reduce energy bills by about 7 – 24 percent compared to non-qualified windows. Your estimated savings will vary depending on current heating and cooling costs in your region.

Multiple Panes

Low E-Coating

Gas Fill

Improved frame materials

Improve comfort. ENERGY STAR qualified windows do more than just lower energy bills; they keep your home's temperature consistently comfortable. During the winter, the interior glass of ENERGY STAR qualified windows stays warmer compared to typical windows, even when the temperature outside dips well below freezing. In the summer, most ENERGY STAR qualified windows reduce the heat gain into your home, without reducing the visible light.

Protect your valuables. Drapes, wood floors, a favorite photograph: all these things can fade or discolor after repeated exposure to direct sunlight. ENERGY STAR qualified windows have coatings that keep out the summer heat and act like sunscreen for your house, protecting your valuables from harmful, fading ultraviolet light without noticeably reducing visible light.

Look for the ENERGY STAR. The ENERGY STAR guidelines for windows are tailored to four climate zones. For example, windows in the North are optimized to reduce heat loss in the winter, while windows in the South are optimized to reduce heat gain during the summer. For optimal results, select ENERGY STAR qualified windows that are appropriate for your climate zone.

Making a Change? Choose the Right Equipment

If you've taken the steps outlined in the previous sections to improve efficiency and you continue to experience problems, or if your HVAC system is old (10 – 15 years) or not working, consider replacing your equipment with a high-efficiency unit that has earned the ENERGY STAR. It's a good idea to do some research on options for a new heating or cooling system before your current one breaks, so you can make an informed decision if you need to act quickly.

How much energy you save will vary based on your use and climate, with colder regions saving more with ENERGY STAR heating equipment and hotter regions saving more with ENERGY STAR cooling equipment.

Furnaces

Furnaces are the most commonly used residential heating system in the United States. Running most often on gas, but sometimes on oil, propane, or electricity, furnaces deliver their heat through a duct system. Furnaces that have earned the ENERGY STAR have higher AFUE (Annual Fuel Utilization Efficiency) ratings. AFUE is the measure of heating equipment efficiency, represented as a percentage. Most furnaces that can qualify for the ENERGY STAR will be "condensing" furnaces where the transfer of heat is so thorough water or condensate is a byproduct of combustion. This condensing occurs with systems over 90 percent efficient. Another feature of efficient furnaces is a highly efficient blower motor (commonly an ECM, Electronically Commutated Motor, or another type of "advanced main air circulating fan").

Boilers

A boiler heats your home by burning gas, propane, or oil to heat water or steam that circulates through radiators, baseboards, or radiant floor systems. Boilers do not use a duct system. Boilers that have earned the ENERGY STAR have higher AFUE ratings. Features that improve boiler efficiency include electronic ignition, which eliminates the need to have the pilot light burning all the time, and technologies that extract more heat from the same amount of fuel.

Central Air Conditioners

Most residential central air conditioners are called "split-systems" because they have an outdoor component with a condenser and compressor and an indoor component with an evaporator coil. It's very important to replace both of these units at the same time. Installing a new outdoor unit without replacing the indoor unit is likely to result in low efficiency, and may lead to premature failure of the system.

ENERGY STAR qualified central air conditioners have higher SEER (Seasonal Energy Efficiency Ratio) and EER (Energy Efficiency Ratio) ratings than today's standard models. SEER is the most commonly used measurement of efficiency for air conditioners. It measures how efficiently a cooling system will operate over an entire season. EER measures how efficiently a cooling system will operate when the outdoor temperature is at a specific level (95 degrees F).

The central air conditioner also needs a blower motor—which is usually part of the furnace—to blow the cool air through the duct system. The only way to ensure that your new air conditioner performs at its rated efficiency, is to replace your heating system at the same time. It's especially recommended if your furnace is over 15 years old. If you purchase a new energy-efficient air conditioner but connect it to an older furnace and blower motor, your system will not perform to its rated efficiency.

Heat Pumps

Heat pumps provide both heating and cooling in one integrated system.

Electric Air-Source Heat Pumps (ASHPs). ASHPs, often used in moderate climates, use the difference between outdoor and indoor air temperatures to cool and heat. ENERGY STAR qualified ASHPs have higher SEER and EER ratings than conventional models. They also have a higher Heating and Seasonal Performance Factor (HSPF), which measures the heating efficiency of the heat pump.

Geothermal Heat Pumps (GHPs). GHPs are similar to air source heat pumps, but use the ground instead of outside air to provide heating, cooling, and often water heating. Because they use the earth's natural heat, they are among the most efficient and comfortable heating and cooling technologies currently available. Although initially expensive, you can achieve significant cost savings on energy bills. GHPs are most often installed in new homes and require a duct system.

ENERGY STAR

Work with a Heating and Cooling Contractor

Whether you want to schedule an annual equipment maintenance check-up or you've decided that you need to purchase and install new heating or cooling equipment, you will need to hire a contractor.

The following sections will help you find the right contractor, get quality and value from the contractor and your new equipment, and get a signed agreement on the work to be done. Many of the following recommendations also apply if you choose to work with a contractor to make other home improvements such as home sealing or duct work.

Choose the Right Contractor

A reputable contractor should:

☐ Perform an on-site inspection of the work you want completed and provide a detailed bid in a timely manner.

☐ Demonstrate to you that the company is licensed and insured to repair and install heating and cooling equipment (many states require this).

☐ Be able to provide his/her certification for refrigerant handling, required since 1992.

☐ Have several years of experience as a business in your community.

☐ Provide examples of quality installation of energy-efficient heating and/or cooling equipment work, with names of customers that you can contact.

☐ Complete and submit the warranty information card on your behalf.

☐ Leave all equipment manuals and provide documentation of installation procedures, including sizing calculations, AHRI certificate, and records of any measurements or testing.

☐ Clearly explain the benefits of regular maintenance and help you set up a schedule to keep your system operating at its best.

Sign an Agreement Before Work Begins
Both you and your contractor should sign a written proposal
before work gets started. The agreement or proposal should:

☐ List in detail all the work that is being contracted and show you a layout of
where the equipment is going to be installed.

☐ Specify all products by quantity, name, model number, and energy ratings.

☐ Provide manufacturer's warranty, equipment documentation, and contractor
installation warranty information (if applicable).

☐ Give the payment schedule.

☐ State the scheduled start and completion date.

☐ Describe how disputes will be resolved.

☐ State the contractor's liability insurance and licenses if required.

☐ Outline paperwork and permits needed for the project.

ENERGY STAR

Get an ENERGY STAR Quality Installation

Replacing your old heating and cooling equipment with new, energy-efficient models is a great start. But to make sure that you get the best performance, the new equipment must be properly installed. In fact, improper installation can reduce system efficiency by up to 30 percent—costing you more on your utility bills and possibly shortening the equipment's life.

Make sure to ask your contractor if his or her work meets ENERGY STAR Quality Installation guidelines. These guidelines, based on the Air Conditioning Contractors of America's (ACCA) quality installation specification, require:

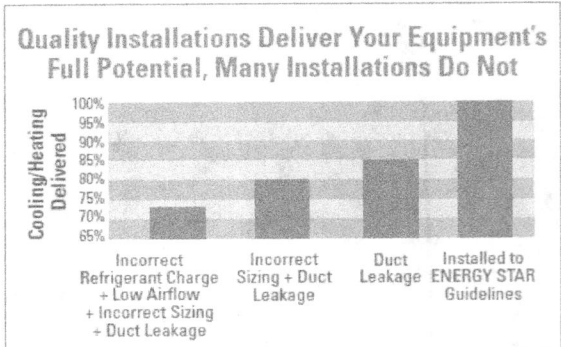

Quality Installations Deliver Your Equipment's Full Potential, Many Installations Do Not

Proper Sizing of Equipment

Installing the right size equipment for the home is essential to getting the best performance and comfort. Many homeowners believe that bigger is always better when buying new heating and cooling equipment. In reality, a system that's too large will not keep your home comfortable because of frequent 'on/off' cycling. Incorrect sizing can also put stress on system components and shorten the equipment's life. With an ENERGY STAR Quality Installation, your contractor will make sure that you get a system that is the right size for your home.

Sealing Ducts

To help ensure that your new system delivers the heated or cooled air to all the rooms of your home, contractors using ENERGY STAR Quality Installation guidelines will evaluate your duct system to identify leaks, and then seal them using mastic, metal-backed tape, or an aerosol-based sealant. In some instances, your contractor may advise you that it is necessary to replace or add ducts.

Ensuring Proper Refrigerant Charge

Incorrect refrigerant level can lower efficiency by 5 – 20 percent and can ultimately cause premature component failure, resulting in costly repairs. With an ENERGY STAR Quality Installation, your contractor will verify that the refrigerant level in the system is correct.

Optimizing Air Flow

If air flow in your heating and cooling system is too high or too low, you may experience comfort problems and higher utility bills. With an ENERGY STAR Quality Installation, your contractor will test air flow and make any needed adjustments for optimal performance.

When purchasing heating and cooling equipment, choosing energy-efficient products is a step in the right direction. However, asking the right questions of your contractor and making sure your equipment is properly sized and installed are also important elements to ensure that your new system performs at optimal efficiency.

Quality Installation Checklist

When installing your new heating and cooling equipment, your contractor should do the following to ensure a quality installation:

☐ Provide adequate room around the equipment for service and maintenance.

☐ Install and set up a programmable thermostat (if not already in use).

☐ Show you how to change the filter(s).

☐ Test and verify proper airflow (if a furnace or heat pump).

☐ Verify that your furnace or boiler has been tested for proper burner operation and proper venting of flue gases. The vent piping should be inspected for leaks or deterioration and repaired or replaced as necessary.

☐ Install a properly matched indoor coil when replacing an outdoor unit. An old coil will not work efficiently with a new outdoor unit.

☐ Confirm that the level of refrigerant charge and the airflow across the indoor coil meets the manufacturer's recommendation. It's estimated that more than 60 percent of central air conditioners are incorrectly charged during installation.

☐ Place the condenser in an area that can be protected from rain, snow, or vegetation, as specified by the manufacturer. If you have a central air conditioning unit, cover your outside equipment during the winter to protect it from snow and ice. Heat pumps need to be left uncovered to properly operate during the winter.

TAKE THE ENERGY STAR PLEDGE.

Post this checklist where it can be a daily reminder to save energy, save money, and help fight global warming with ENERGY STAR. Then go to energystar.gov/changetheworld and tell us the steps you plan to take.

AT HOME, I PLEDGE TO:

- ☐ Change a Light: Replace at least one light in my home with an ENERGY STAR qualified one. Buy ENERGY STAR qualified holiday lights.
- ☐ Choose ENERGY STAR qualified products: TV, DVD player, home theater in a box (sound system), clothes washer, dishwasher, refrigerator.
- ☐ Choose ENERGY STAR qualified equipment for my home office: computer, monitor, multi-function device, fax, ink-jet printer.
- ☐ Enable my ENERGY STAR computer and monitor to sleep while I'm away.
- ☐ Set or program my thermostat to save energy while I'm asleep or away from home.
- ☐ Have my heating and cooling equipment tuned-up by a professional and change my air filter.
- ☐ Seal obvious leaks and repair disconnections in my home's duct system.
- ☐ Seal my home's envelope (outer walls, ceiling, windows, doors, and floors) with caulk, spray foam, and weather stripping, and add insulation to the attic.

AT WORK, I PLEDGE TO:

- ☐ Use a power strip as a central turn off point for all my office equipment to completely disconnect from the power supply.
- ☐ Unplug electronics once they are charged.
- ☐ Keep air vents clear of paper, files, and office supplies.
- ☐ Create a Green Team with my co-workers to help build support for energy efficiency.
- ☐ Talk to my boss about earning EPA's ENERGY STAR for our building.

The U.S. Environmental Protection Agency encourages everyone to save money and fight global warming through energy-efficient products and practices. Learn more at energystar.gov.